The Life of a
BUTTERFLY

Clare Hibbert

www.raintreepublishers.co.uk

Visit our website to find out more information about **Raintree** books.

To order:
- ☎ Phone 44 (0) 1865 888112
- 📄 Send a fax to 44 (0) 1865 314091
- 💻 Visit the Raintree Bookshop at **www.raintreepublishers.co.uk** to browse our catalogue and order online.

First published in Great Britain by Raintree, Halley Court, Jordan Hill, Oxford OX2 8EJ, part of Harcourt Education.
Raintree is a registered trademark of Harcourt Education Ltd.

© Harcourt Education Ltd 2004
First published in paperback in 2005
The moral right of the proprietor has been asserted.

Editorial: Nick Hunter and Catherine Clarke
Design: Michelle Lisseter and Tipani Design (www.tipani.co.uk)
Illustration: Tony Jones, Art Construction
Picture Research: Maria Joannou and Ginny Stroud-Lewis
Production: Jonathan Smith

Originated by Dot Gradations Ltd
Printed and bound in China by South China Printing Company

ISBN 1 844 43315 3 (hardback)
08 07 06 05 04
10 9 8 7 6 5 4 3 2 1

ISBN 1 844 43322 6 (paperback)
09 08 07 06 05
10 9 8 7 6 5 4 3 2 1

British Library Cataloguing in Publication Data
Hibbert, Clare
The Life of a Butterfly. – (Life Cycles)
571.8′15789
A full catalogue record for this book is available from the British Library.

Acknowledgements
The publishers would like to thank the following for permission to reproduce photographs:
Alamy Images p.**29**; Ardea pp.**24** (Alan Weaving), **25** (Jim Zipp); Corbis (Anthony Bannister/Gallo Images) p.**22**; Fotonatura pp.**12** (Frans Lanting, MP), **23** (Jim Brandenburg, MP); Getty Images pp.**15** (Botanica), **27** (Taxi); Nature Picture Library pp. **18**, **28** (Nigel Marven); NHPA pp.**4** (T. Kitchin V. Hurst), **5** (Dr Eckart Pott), **17** (John Shaw), **19** (John Shaw), **20** (John Shaw); Oxford Scientific Films pp. **8**, **9** (Breck P. Kent), **10**, **11**, **13** (Michael Fogden), **14** (Breck P. Kent), **16** (Mantis Wildlife Films), **26** (Chris Sharp); Science Photo Library (Susumu Nishinaga) p.**21**.

Cover photograph of a monarch butterfly, reproduced with permission of Premaphotos Wildlife (Jean Preston Mafham).

The publishers would like to thank Janet Stott for her assistance in the preparation of this book.

Every effort has been made to contact copyright holders of any material reproduced in this book. Any omissions will be rectified in subsequent printings if notice is given to the publishers.

The paper used to print this book comes from sustainable resources.

Contents

Any words appearing in bold, **like this**, are explained
in the Glossary.

The butterfly

Butterflies are insects. The adults have beautiful, colourful wings. Like all insects, a butterfly has three sections to its body, six legs, and a pair of feelers called **antennae**. Baby butterflies look nothing like their parents. They are called caterpillars.

This is an adult monarch butterfly. Its wings are orange, white and black.

antenna

head

wing

leg

Growing up

Just as you grow bigger year by year, a butterfly grows and changes, too. All these changes happen in just a few weeks or months. There are many different types of butterfly, but they all have the same basic **life cycle**. This book is about the life cycle of the monarch butterfly.

Where in the world?

Butterflies are found almost all over the world. Monarch butterflies live in North and South America, Australia and some Pacific islands, including Hawaii.

There are hundreds of monarch butterflies in this photograph.

A butterfly's life

The **life cycle** of a butterfly begins when a female lays an egg. A few days later, a tiny caterpillar **hatches** from the egg. Over the next few weeks, the caterpillar grows to more than five times its original size. Then, it is ready to turn into its adult form – a butterfly with wings. It does this inside a special hard casing called a **chrysalis**.

The length of a life

Most monarchs live for two to four weeks as adults. Butterflies born late in the summer live as adults for about five months or more. These special monarchs fly south for winter. They do not **mate** or lay their eggs until the following spring.

After a few days, a caterpillar hatches from the egg.

The caterpillar grows bigger. It sheds its skin four times.

The female butterfly lays her eggs on a leaf.

At about three weeks, the caterpillar turns into a **pupa**.

Adult butterflies mate after three to eight days.

Ten to twelve days later, a butterfly emerges.

This diagram shows the life cycle of a butterfly, from egg to adult.

Laying eggs

Monarch butterflies **mate** and lay eggs between early spring and late summer. The female monarch lays her small, oval eggs on milkweed plants. Often, she lays a single egg on each plant so that when the egg **hatches**, the caterpillar will have a whole plant to itself.

This monarch butterfly is laying one of her eggs on a milkweed plant.

Sticky stuff

The female sticks each egg to the underside of a leaf with a dab of glue. The glue comes out of her body at the same time as the egg. Underneath the leaf, the egg will have shelter from the sun and rain. It will also be hidden from hungry birds and other **predators**.

Milkweed

Milkweed stems are full of milky, **poisonous sap**. Most animals are put off by its bitter taste, but not the monarch caterpillar. It will only eat milkweed. The poisons do not harm the caterpillar – they even help to protect it. They make the caterpillar's body so poisonous that most birds will not try to eat it.

This photograph has been highly **magnified**. Really, each butterfly's egg is no bigger than a pinhead.

9

Egg story

The tiny butterfly egg has a hard, ridged shell and a waxy lining. These protect the miniature caterpillar inside, and stop it from drying out.

Inside the egg, the caterpillar grows bigger until it is ready to **hatch**. You can tell that changes are going on inside the egg because it changes colour. When it is laid, the egg is yellowish-white. Over the next few days, it turns dark grey.

This egg is around five days old. The dark blob at the top is the caterpillar's head.

Ready to hatch

After three to five days, you can see the black head of the caterpillar inside the egg. It is ready to hatch. The little, stripy caterpillar chews a hole in the egg and wriggles out. It is less than 1 centimetre long. The first thing it does is eat the leftover eggshell – it is full of **nutrients**!

How many legs?

An adult butterfly has three pairs of legs attached to its **thorax**. The caterpillar has these, too. It also has five extra pairs of legs, called **prolegs**. It will lose these when it changes into an adult.

The newly-hatched caterpillar makes short work of eating up its shell.

Shedding skin

As the caterpillar eats, its body gets plumper. Just as you outgrow old clothes, the caterpillar is soon too big for its own skin. Starting at the head, its skin splits along its body. There is a brand new stripey skin waiting underneath. At first it is soft and saggy, but it soon moulds itself to the caterpillar's body. The caterpillar gobbles up the old skin and then carries on looking for juicy leaves.

The stripey caterpillar eats milkweed flowers as well as leaves.

Moulting

This way of shedding skin is called **moulting**. The caterpillar moults four times in total, about every five days. At each new stage its body is bigger than before. The bigger the caterpillar grows, the bigger it will be as an adult butterfly.

Parasites

Some tiny types of fly and wasp lay their eggs under the skin of monarch caterpillars. When the eggs hatch, the young wasp **larvae** feed on the caterpillar's flesh. Eventually the caterpillar dies. Animals that live off the bodies of other animals like this are called parasites.

Parasites live off all types of caterpillar, not just the monarch. This poor caterpillar is covered with tiny pink **chrysalises**. Each one has a wasp **pupa** inside.

Hungry and hunted

The monarch caterpillar is a munching machine! It eats night and day and can get through a milkweed leaf in less than five minutes. It also likes to feed on milkweed flowers.

The caterpillar has jaws, or mandibles, to bite through the milkweed leaves.

Avoiding predators

A juicy caterpillar makes a tempting meal for many animals. Luckily, the monarch's bold stripes are a warning that it is **poisonous**. Most frogs, lizards, mice and birds stay away. They prefer to pick on types of caterpillar that are not poisonous. A few animals, however, have found ways to deal with the poison. Stink bugs, wasps and spiders all hunt and eat monarch caterpillars.

Caterpillar senses

The caterpillar does not rely on sight to find food. Although it has six pairs of eyes, they are small and weak. Instead, the caterpillar feels its way, using its pair of short **antennae**. The tiny hairs along its body are also sensitive.

The caterpillar waves its antennae as it moves along. They help it to sense the world around it.

Last moult

Now the caterpillar is about a month old and has grown to 5 centimetres long. It has finally stopped eating. It is about to pupate – turn into a **pupa**. It needs to do this so that it can change into an adult butterfly. First, the caterpillar finds the underside of a branch. Next, it spins some silk from its **spinneret**, just like a spider. Using the sticky silk, it fixes its **abdomen** to the branch. Once it is hanging upside down, it **moults** for the last time.

The caterpillar hangs in the shape of a letter 'J'. A blob of sticky silk holds it to the branch.

The pupa

The new skin underneath is different to the others. When it dries, it looks glassy. It is bright green with specks of gold. This hard case, called a **chrysalis**, will protect the pupa while it is changing into a butterfly.

Slowly the caterpillar's skin splits. Underneath, the chrysalis looks milky at first.

The pupa

While it is inside the **chrysalis**, the **pupa** turns into a butterfly. Its whole body breaks down into a soft mush. The body then rebuilds itself into a butterfly.

Changing names

This way of changing is called metamorphosis. Because the caterpillar has to make a total change in order to become a butterfly, it is called a complete metamorphosis.

At first, once it has hardened, the chrysalis looks bright green.

Some insect babies, such as grasshopper nymphs, already look a bit like their parents. They only have to change a little, so this is called an incomplete metamorphosis.

The metamorphosis from caterpillar to butterfly takes ten to twelve days. Near the end of this time, you can just see the orange, white and black wings of the butterfly inside the chrysalis.

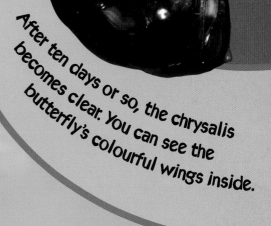

After ten days or so, the chrysalis becomes clear. You can see the butterfly's colourful wings inside.

Sudden movements

The pupa is fixed to a branch and cannot move – but there is sometimes movement inside the pupa. This happens if the pupa is disturbed. It must mean that the pupa can sense the world around it.

A butterfly emerges

When it is time for the butterfly to come out of the **chrysalis**, the skin of the chrysalis splits open. The butterfly comes out very slowly. It is limp and damp with crumpled wings.

After it wriggles out of the chrysalis, the butterfly must wait for a few hours before it is strong enough to fly.

Sunbathing butterfly

The monarch pumps blood into the veins inside its wings so that they straighten out. It basks in the sunshine, drying its body. It can take a few hours before the butterfly is ready to fly. Like all flying insects, the butterfly knows how to fly by **instinct**. It flutters high into the air and glides along on the breeze.

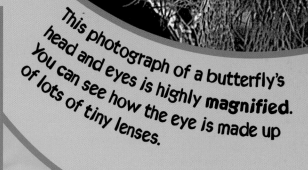

This photograph of a butterfly's head and eyes is highly **magnified**. You can see how the eye is made up of lots of tiny lenses.

Eyesight

As a caterpillar, the monarch had very poor sight, but its adult eyes are amazing. The butterfly has two **compound eyes** – the surface of each eye is made up of hundreds of six-sided **lenses**. Butterflies can even see some colours that humans cannot.

Feeding

Now that it is an adult, the butterfly will not grow any bigger. It still needs food, however, so that it can fly and **mate**. The adult butterfly has a mouthpart like a drinking straw, called a proboscis. Most of the time this is coiled up, but it unfurls when the butterfly drinks.

The butterfly uses its proboscis like a drinking straw to suck up the nectar from the flower.

proboscis

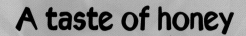

A taste of honey

The butterfly drinks water and sweet **nectar** from flowers, which it sniffs out using its **antennae**. The butterfly has a scaly, hairy taste bud, called a palp, on each side of the proboscis. The palp tells the butterfly whether a liquid is safe to drink.

Pollination

A flower produces nectar to attract butterflies and bees. As the insect drinks the sugary liquid, it brushes against yellow grains of pollen, which stick to its body. The pollen may rub off on to the next flower the butterfly visits. A flower needs pollen from another flower in order to make seeds – so the insects are helping with the flower's **life cycle**.

Sometimes, pollen sticks to the butterfly's wings. It rubs off when the butterfly visits another flower.

Finding a mate

When the adult butterfly is three to eight days old, it is ready to **mate**. Butterflies need to mate so that they can have young. The male butterfly gives off a special scent. This smell will attract a female. She senses it with her **antennae** and comes closer to mate.

The male and female mate by joining the ends of their abdomens.

Joined together

To mate, the butterflies join the tips of their **abdomens**. They stay like this for up to sixteen hours. A female only needs to mate once. After this, all of her hundreds of eggs are **fertile** – each of them could grow into a baby caterpillar.

Males and females

You can tell a male monarch from a female monarch by looking at the wings. Females are usually slightly darker, while males have a dark spot on each back wing. There is another difference, too. The end of the female's abdomen is more pointed – better shaped for laying eggs.

The butterfly on the bottom right of this photograph is a male. It has a black blob on each back wing.

Migration

A monarch butterfly that comes out of its **chrysalis** at the end of the summer is different. It looks like an adult, but it cannot **mate** or lay eggs. That is because the milkweed is dying and there would not be any food for the caterpillars.

Flying south

To survive the cold winter, these monarchs make a special journey. This is called migration.

These butterflies have journeyed to Mexico. They are resting on the bark of a fir tree.

The butterflies fly south to California or Mexico – warm places where there are flowers with **nectar** to drink. Thousands of monarchs gather and live together at these sites. The journey takes one or two months. The monarchs use the position of the Sun in the sky to help find their way. Monarchs are the most famous migrating butterflies. Others include painted ladies and red admirals. Most butterflies, however, do not migrate at all.

The red admiral butterfly can be found in North America, Europe and North Africa. It flies south for winter.

Picky bird

An adult monarch contains **poison** from the milkweed it ate as a caterpillar. Some creatures can eat monarchs without being poisoned. The black-backed oriole is a bird that lives in Mexico. It leaves the poisonous parts of the butterfly – its wings and skin – and gobbles up the rest.

Flying home

When spring comes, the days become longer and warmer. This tells the monarch butterflies that it is time to fly north. It also makes changes in their bodies. They are able to **mate**.

Up, up and away! The butterflies take to the skies and head north.

New beginnings

Once she has mated, the female can lay her eggs – about 700 of them. First she checks that she has chosen a milkweed plant. She drums her six legs against the stem of the plant. Special **sense organs** on her leg can tell her if it is a milkweed plant. If it is, she chooses a leaf and glues one egg underneath. In a few days the egg will **hatch**. A tiny monarch caterpillar will crawl out and the **life cycle** can begin all over again.

Inside each egg are the beginnings of a new life.

Ends... and beginnings

Mating is such hard work for the males that they die soon afterwards. Once the females have laid all their eggs, they also die. Every female leaves behind hundreds of eggs, each of which may hatch to create a brand new butterfly life.

Find out for yourself

The best way to find out more about the **life cycle** of a butterfly is to watch it happen with your own eyes. In spring, look on the undersides of leaves and see if you can spot a butterfly's eggs. You can find out more by reading books about butterflies, and by looking for information on the Internet.

Books to read

An Extraordinary Life: The Story of a Monarch Butterfly, Laurence Pringle (Orchard Books, 1997)

DK Readers: Born to be a Butterfly, Karen Wallace (Dorling Kindersley, 2000)

Life Cycles: Butterflies and Other Insects, Sally Morgan (Belitha Press, 2001)

Using the Internet

Explore the Internet to find out more about butterflies. Websites can change, but if one of the links below no longer works, don't worry. Use a search engine such as www.yahooligans.com, and type in keywords such as 'butterfly', 'caterpillar' and 'life cycle'.

Websites

http://www.enchantedlearning.com/subjects/butterfly
More information, activities and printouts to do with butterflies.

http://www.monarchbutterflyusa.com
This is a great site with animations, photos and facts!

Glossary

abdomen tail-end of an insect's body

antennae insect's feelers

chrysalis case enclosing the pupa of a butterfly

compound eye special insect eye made up of hundreds of lenses

fertile describes an egg that will be able to hatch

hatch when a young animal comes out of its egg

instinct behaviour that does not have to be learned

larva young insect that looks nothing like its parent and will have to make some big changes to reach its adult form

lens something that can change the direction of beams of light

life cycle all the different stages in the life of a living thing, such as an animal or plant

magnify to make something look much larger than its actual size

mate when a male and a female come together to make babies

moult lose outer casing, skin or hair

nectar sugary food that flowers make to attract insects

nutrients parts of food that the body needs to live

poison something that will cause illness or death if eaten

pollination when male pollen from one flower is carried to another flower. This has to happen before a seed can start to grow.

predator animal that hunts other animals and eats them for food

proleg one of the legs that caterpillars have, but not butterflies

pupa insect going through the stage between larva and adult

sap juice inside a plant's leaves and stems

sense organs parts of the body such as eyes and ears that receive information from the outside world

spinneret organ that produces silk, found on a caterpillar's lip

thorax middle, chest part of an insect's body

Index